The Massey Lectures are co-sponsored by Massey College, in the University of Toronto, and CBC Radio. The series was created in honour of the Right Honourable Vincent Massey, former governor general of Canada, and was inaugurated in 1961 to enable distinguished authorities to communicate the results of original study or research on a variety of subjects of contemporary interest.

This book is based on the five-part 1984 Massey Lectures of the same name, which were broadcast in December 1984 as part of CBC Radio's *Ideas* series. The executive producer of the series was Bernie Lucht.

LATIN AMERICA

AT WAR WITH THE PAST

CARLOS FUENTES

Published in 2001 by
House of Anansi Press Limited
895 Don Mills Rd., 400-2 Park Centre
Toronto, ON, M3C 1W3
Tel. (416) 445-3333
Fax (416) 445-5967
www.anansi.ca

Distributed in Canada by
General Distribution Services Ltd.
325 Humber College Blvd.
Etobicoke, ON, M9W 7C3
Tel. (416) 213-1919
Fax (416) 213-1917
E-mail cservice@genpub.com

First published in 1985 by CBC Enterprises
CBC logo used with permission

05 04 03 02 01   2 3 4 5 6

National Library of Canada Cataloguing in Publication Data

Fuentes, Carlos
Latin America : at war with the past

(CBC Massey lectures ; 1984)
ISBN 0-88784-665-3

1. Latin America — History. 2. Latin America — Foreign relations — United States. 3. United States — Foreign relations — Latin America.
I. Title.
II. Series: CBC Massey lectures series

F1410.F83 2001   980   C00-933189-1

Cover Design: Bill Douglas @ The Bang

We acknowledge for their financial support of our publishing program the Canada Council for the Arts, the Ontario Arts Council, and the Government of Canada through the Book Publishing Industry Development Program (BPIDP).

Printed and bound in Canada

LATIN AMERICA

inequality poverty war

freedoms from freedoms from intervention

vs. ↑

free trade lack of social programs

effects of globalization

Cuba

Columbia

Chile: - inequality ↑

- stable economy (Pinochet)

- political fear

Nicaragua

I

ONE of my earliest photographic memories is of my father, a young man of twenty-five with horn-rimmed glasses and a straw boater, straddling the Mexican-American border at towns with hot, dusty names: Laredo/Nuevo Laredo; El Paso/Ciudad Juárez; Nogales, Arizona/Nogales, Sonora.

He had just started his career as a freshman lawyer on the Mexican-American Border Claims Commission, created in the mid-twenties, in the wake of the Mexican Revolution, to listen to the grievances of Americans affected by Pancho Villa's incursions into New Mexico and of Mexicans affected by "Black Jack" Pershing's incursions into Chihuahua as Pershing searched in vain for Villa in mountains that the Mexican revolutionist knew like the back of his hand.

This image of my father standing with one foot in Mexico and the other in the United States became a picture of my own self, a symbol of my own imagination.

The three-thousand-mile border between Mexico and the United States is more than a border between Mexico and the United States: it is the border between the United States and all of Latin America, for Latin America begins at the Mexican border.

It is the only frontier between the industrialized and the developing worlds.

It is the frontier between two memories: a memory of triumph and a memory of loss, best expressed by Mexican dictator Porfirio Díaz's famous exclamation: "Poor Mexico! So far from God and so near to the United States!"

It is the frontier between two cultures: the Protestant, capitalist, Nordic culture, and the southern, Indo-Mediterranean, Catholic culture of syncretism and the baroque.

Our faces see themselves across this frontier, which then becomes the frontier each one of us carries within him.

Every Latin American has a personal frontier with the United States.

And every North American, before this century, is over, will find that he or she has a personal frontier with Latin America.

This is a living frontier, which can be nourished by information but, above all, by knowledge, by understanding, by the pursuit of enlightened self-interest on both parts.

Or it can be starved by suspicion, ghost stories, arrogance, ignorance, scorn and violence.

We are here today to explore both possibilities.

When I was speaking recently with the Mexican poet Octavio Paz on this and other matters, he said that there would always be problems between Latin America and the United States, even if the relationship of power were drastically changed and the Americans became weak while we became strong.

The problems would persist because the two cultures are so different, so dissimilar in their origins, so strange to each other and therefore so challenging to the comprehension of the other side.

We are different, we are other: North Americans (by which I mean only the citizens of the United States) and Latin Americans.

But we cannot impose our vision of the world on the United States, nor can they on us.

We must try to bridge our differences without denying them:

We are worried about redeeming the past.
They are accustomed to acclaiming the future.

Their past is assimilated; and, too often, it is simply forgotten.
Ours is still battling for our souls.

We represent the abundance of poverty.
They, the poverty of abundance.

They want to live better.
We want to die better.

North Americans are accustomed to success.
Latin Americans, to failure.

Or, rather, the unaccustomed failures of the North Americans drive them first to a self-flagellating malaise of incomprehension before striking back blindly to prove their strength, to stand tall and to feel that God has singled them out.

We measure our scarce successes with the sad misgivings of experience; all things in life are limited and fleeting, especially success.

North Americans are, religiously, the children of the heretic Pelagius, who believed in direct Grace between God and Man.

We are descendants of the orthodox Saint Augustine, who believed that Grace is achieved only through the mediation of hierarchy.

The *gringos* are founded on the parsimony of the Protestant work ethic.

We, in Latin America, on autocratic dispensation and baroque prodigality.

North Americans save.

We squander.

North Americans peer at their ledgers through the spectacles of Ben Franklin.

We spend our wealth on ceremonies, altars and cemeteries, like Philip II of Spain.

The United States has practised horizontal and extensive decentralization of power.

Latin America has suffered its absolutist, pyramidal and centralized oppressions.

The North belongs to the tradition of the customary, unwritten law — the Common Law.

The South, to the Roman legal tradition, in which nothing exists unless it is written.

The United States was born in perfect consonance with the values of modernity: the wedlock of religion and economics; free enterprise; free inquiry; self-government; scepticism; criticism; division of powers, checks and balances; federalism.

Latin America was born in perfect discord with those same values: dogmatism; royal absolutism; the refusal of modernity; centralism; the Holy Inquisition; the decision to prolong the Holy Roman order and its mediaeval imperium; the divorce between the religious man and the economic man; rigid ecclesiastical societies.

Gertrude Stein called the United States "the oldest country in the world"; the oldest simply because it was the first to be new; the oldest modern democracy; the first modern nation.

Since independence from Spain was achieved in the 1820s, Latin America, too, has sought, at all costs, to be modern: to give birth to democratic, prosperous, free nations.

But none of these values has been created magically by the laws that invoked them. Democracy, freedom, prosperity — the *legal* country — have been hard to come by without somehow modifying the structural factors of the past — the *real* country.

Nature and history have been kind to the United States:

Vast natural resources.

Navigable rivers.

No peasantry; independent farmers.

No Middle Ages; no feudalism.

Only two neighbours, and both of them weak.

But a heavy cross of crucified flesh to bear, an insufferable contradiction to the values of equality and modernity:

Slavery, racial repugnance, segregation.

Latin America has not had to deal with a comparable problem on the bloody revolutionary scale that the United States had to in the 1860s. But we have had to deal with just as much patriotic gore and civil strife against other problems, derived from our own historical tradition.

Leafing through a now-forgotten document, the report of the Kissinger Commission on Central America, I was struck by the reporter's insistence on differentiating between "indigenous" revolutions in this hemisphere — that is, the American and Mexican revolutions — and "non-indigenous," imported or exotic revolutions, that is, those in Cuba and Nicaragua.

I was intrigued by this distinction.

First, because it is hard to conceive of the American Revolution without outside aid.

Second, because the report hails the Mexican Revolution without remembering that it was every bit as harassed by the United States governments, from Taft to Hoover, as the Cubans and Nicaraguans have been in our own time.

Third, because it would like Central America to achieve the results of the Mexican Revolution without having to go through the mess of the Mexican Revolution, which still is, after the American Civil War, the bloodiest revolution this hemisphere has witnessed.

Fourth, because of the unabashed historical amnesia that runs through the report, and through most North American policy decisions on Latin America.

And fifth, finally, and perhaps most important, because, while reading it, I reflected that the only things truly indigenous to Latin America were theocratic Indian empires; religious intolerance and inquisition; Spanish royal authoritarianism; and a sort of backlands, repressive patrimonialism of a most primitive nature.

Capitalism and Communism seem to me rather secondary, derivative and cosmetic references in view of the persistence of our founding characteristics.

The Iberian New World, born with the promise of Utopia, imagined by Renaissance Europe to be the privileged space of the Golden Age and the Noble Savage, where the West would cleanse its sins of war, greed and apostasy, has carried the burden of happiness even as history has denied it almost constantly, not only to Latin Americans but to the majority of mankind.

What a heavy load: to bear the cross of Utopia as Utopia was made impossible by the conquerors and colonizers of Utopia!

Yes, Latin America has been touched by defeat: the epic denial of Utopia by the conquest and the colony, the enstatement of rigid, dogmatic, vertically ordained structures of power and religion.

We have struggled mightily with these root realities. We are at war with them — we are at war with ourselves, not with the United States — and we must solve these problems by ourselves, not through artificial confrontations in an East/West context.

Yes, we have learned through our experience that all things in life are fleeting and insecure, especially happiness, especially success.

Yet we have lived next door to the biggest success story of modernity: the United States of America, the country that will not admit defeat or the limits of power, the democratic empire struggling with its dual nature — Jekyll and Hyde.

Yes, we are separated by our different cultures more than by our different power.

Yes, the United States has wanted to possess the future.

Yes, Latin America has wanted to redeem the past.

Yet we must share the present, and it is a conflictive one.

Latin America is living through one of the greatest crises — some say the greatest — of its whole history.

Our road to modernity has been rocky.

Democracy and prosperity have not always responded to the laws that invoked them; nor, when achieved, have their benefits been evenly distributed.

But during the past 160 years, and especially since the end of World War Two, Latin America has managed to expand economically, to accumulate wealth, to give rise to modern social classes and to extend certain limited benefits of health and education to its population.

The sense of the crisis we are living through today is that it endangers even these modest gains and puts the whole question of our modern viability into doubt.

Increasing material wealth without equivalent social distribution is giving way to a decrease in wealth and a decrease in justice:

The middle classes are increasingly restless as they undergo a revolution of lost expectations.

The rural areas are increasingly poor as prices for agricultural products steadily decline.

The search for diversified sources of economic and technological support decreases.

The cycle of debt-fuelled development has now come full cycle to a situation of debt-fuelled stagnation:

The foreign debt of Latin America stands at three hundred fifty billion dollars.

Its export earnings have come down to ninety-five billion dollars a year.

Two-thirds of the debt is owed to commercial banks.

Interest payments to these banks now equal forty-eight percent of export earnings.

In 1983, Latin America paid forty billion dollars in interest.

So Latin America has become a net exporter of capital when it needs it most.

Each time the rate of interest in the United States jumps by one percentage point, two and a half billion dollars are added to our foreign debt.

In 1982, exports from the Third World to the industrialized world declined by forty-two billion dollars.

But imports to the Third World from the industrialized nations fell accordingly: in the case of Mexico alone, we imported seven billion dollars less from the United States in 1983.

All of this directly affects the economy of the United States, indeed, of the whole West.

It affects the stability of banks, whose Latin American debt sometimes comes perilously close to being equal to half, three-quarters or even more than its total capital resources.

It affects export-related job losses, which accounted for forty percent of United States unemployment between 1980 and 1982. By the end of 1984, this could cost the American economy as many as one and a half million jobs.

Not only the United States, but indeed the whole world, and certainly Latin America, faces what Eliot Janeway calls "a financial Pearl Harbor."

And the millions of urban marginals in our great cities, depoliticized, with nothing to lose, festering in the *favelas* and *ranchos*, in the *ciudades perdidas*, the lost cities, prepare their assault on the citadels of wealth and privilege: I fear we might plunge into a millenarist explosion of mediaeval resonances in Latin America.

Bereft of political structure, a movement such as this could be quickly co-opted by messianic demagogues and appeal to the abiding sense of religious fervour: *a consecration of violence*.

For religion and violence are ingrained in the culture of Latin America; they do not have to be taught. And they finally strengthen yet another Latin American tradition: the authoritarian uses — and abuses — of power.

I hope we have political answers to these dangers.

I hope we have rational answers to the problem of the ecological disruption of our cities and our great natural forests and river basins; of the barely controlled demographic explosion; of the standstill of social programs that cannot be paid for in the present circumstances; of our growing need for importing food; of our increasing crime rate.

All of this is now reflected in the price riots in the Dominican Republic, in the invasion of supermarkets in Rio de Janeiro, in the lynching of criminals in the *favelas* of São Paulo. These are things that shall also happen in Mexico City, the capital of underdevelopment, and in Caracas, surrounded by miserable *ranchos*; in Bogotá, the capital of drugs and beggars, and in Lima, besieged by the ayatollahs of the Shining Path. Everywhere.

All of this would be a far greater danger to the security of the United States than the politics of two and a half million Nicaraguans. This is what should be concentrating our attention and our will, not the illegal arming of contras under CIA patronage, nor the publication of counter-revolutionary primers on how to "neutralize" Sandinista officials or how to stuff toilets in Managua.

Yet both superpowers are unable to face change within their traditional spheres of influence and blame each other for the internal dynamics of Nicaragua or Poland, introducing the East/West conflict into regional problematics and adding the dangers of a generalized war to the mounting social, political and economic crisis.

We should be clearing the decks for action: clearing them of minor problems that can be solved through diplomacy, never through war; revising the terms of our common economic interests and even drafting local revolutionary movements to assist in throwing overboard the dead weight — not the living matter — of the historical inheritance I have mentioned here.

We should be studying calls for a new Breton Woods conference, such as the one being made by Andrew Young since 1979.

We should be listening to Peru's Pédro Pablo Kuczynski, when he counsels that just as negotiated settlements are needed to deal with political problems, so a negotiated economic settlement is urgently required. In the long run, he says, the resources to repay the debt are there. "But there will have to be some formula that reduces the interest burden below the forty billion dollars that it was last year," he adds.

Just such a formula has been offered by Britain's Harold Lever. Lord Lever urges the world financial community to give debtors a breathing space, deferring current interest for the sake of future profit through new no-interest securities, which would transform short-term debt into medium- and long-term instruments to finance productive investment.

The current situation is the co-responsibility of euphoric and sometimes corrupt Latin governments and international banks hurriedly ridding themselves of petro-dollars and seeking collateral El Dorados in this hemisphere.

The sum of the Latin foreign debt is exactly the same as the sum of dollars stashed away by private Latin Americans in foreign banks.

The temptation to form a debtors' club and declare a moratorium has been avoided several times. Can it be forever postponed? It would wreak havoc on an international monetary system already severely undermined by Western refusals to consider seriously the North/South negotiations and by the vagaries of United States monetary policies — deficits and high interest rates — and commercial policies implemented without due consideration of their effects on Third World nations.

Latin America does not require war games in Central America.

It requires initiatives furthering co-development in an interdependent world.

We all agree that the world economic crisis will only be solved in co-operation, not in isolation.

The principal areas of co-development are universally proclaimed: We must co-operate in energy, trade, food production and financial affairs.

What must be clearly understood is that the developing nations are not acting as supplicants in these matters. Solutions are vital to both developed and developing countries.

The developing world is suffering from inflation with unemployment and slow growth, shrinking services, declining standards of living and exacerbations of social intolerance.

These problems will not be solved by transitory, theatrical exercises in voodoo economics: deficits shall be paid, if not today, then tomorrow; if not by the fathers, then by the children.

A major world power cannot liquidate its foreign investments, year after year, so as not to pay taxes at home and continue to spend more than it earns.

A major world economic power cannot refuse the discipline it happily imposes on emerging Third World nations. And it cannot continue to absorb the capital of the Third World countries in order to avoid facing its own deficits without disastrous consequences for both the developed and the developing worlds.

The developing world is suffering from extreme dependency on exports, lack of public capital for infrastructure, the gigantic debt burden and a growing incapacity to buy what the industrialized nations produce, therefore impoverishing both themselves and the industrialized world. If we cannot buy what we need in order to produce, nor sell what we need for our growth, we shall be condemned to vegetate as potential — never effective — economic units.

Our crisis shall mirror your own Western crisis, since you in the developed world will also stagnate, for lack of growing, confident clients.

The new world economic order is not an exercise in philanthropy but in enlightened self-interest for everyone concerned.

Through rational co-operation, the world economy can re-awaken: this is only possible if social and economic conditions are created for elevating demand and productivity in the developing nations.

You see to what extent we are interdependent.

These are enormous challenges to the United States and, indeed, to Canada and to the EEC nations —

challenges to the West's capacity for diplomacy, to its renewal of the will and the imagination that once directed its energies, and, even more basically, to its intellectual resources, its available information, its knowledge of its own history and of the history of the emerging nations it must deal with.

For without that knowledge, there is no information, no will, no imagination, no diplomacy and no economic system that can finally sustain itself.

While the United States is hypnotically fixed on the problems of the Central American isthmus, suddenly discovered as if they had not been there for several hundred years, the larger problems of Latin America fester and remain explosively latent.

I shall be studying, in the next two lectures, the historical and cultural context from which these problems arise: they are the problems of a continent at odds with itself, with its past, with its unresolved conflicts.

II

THE Year of the Reed, Ce Acatl in the Aztec calendar, 1519 in the Christian chronology, rose ominously over the capital of the Aztec Empire, Tenochtitlán, present-day Mexico City.

Comets streaked for long hours across the sky.

The waters on which the city, an Indian Venice, was built churned up gigantic waves, toppling houses and towers.

The mirrors of the kingdom reflected starry skies at noon.

Strange women roamed the streets at midnight, sobbing over the coming deaths of their children and the fall of the empire.

Dreamers dreamed of apocalypse.

The Aztec emperor, Moctezuma, had all the dreamers brought to his court, there to repeat their dreams aloud. Once they had done so, they were all violently put to death.

If the dreamers were killed, the dreams would not take place: by killing the dreamers, Moctezuma hoped to kill the future.

But in one of the strangest coincidences in history, that future did arrive, precisely in the year foreseen for the return of the blond, bearded God Quetzalcoatl, the plumed serpent, the God of creation, the good God who had given men maize, taught them the arts and, having fallen into temptation, fled to the East but promised to return: in peace, if his children had cared for the earth peacefully; and in war, if they had devastated the land and oppressed other human beings.

For the ancient myth recalled that the earth had not been given to men by the Gods; men were not the owners of this earth, but its gardeners.

The mythic world of pre-Columbian civilizations was not able to meet the challenge of the God Quetzalcoatl as he returned, blond, bearded, on floating houses, riding snorting mythological beasts and spouting fire from his mouth.

This was a sacred world, fearful of the chaos of the world being born and of the violence of the world coming to an end.

It sustained the fragile universe through human sacrifice, feeding the sun with blood: otherwise, it might never rise again.

It honoured the sun through an art of cosmic, barbaric figures that have survived their theological inception and today speak to us, in contemporary terms, of fear, of the yearning for unity and of the transitoriness of human endeavour.

This Indian conception of the world asserted itself through vertical, authoritarian and militarist powers.

It met the challenge of a nation that could no longer contain itself within its borders. Spain, riding on the militaristic dynamics of the prolonged war against the Moors, had united under the dual monarchy of the Catholic rulers, Ferdinand and Isabella:

It had conquered the last stronghold of Islam in Spain, the kingdom of Granada;

It had expelled the Jews from Spain;

It had revived the Holy Inquisition, strengthening it under the power of the Crown;

And it had discovered, thanks to the genius of Christopher Columbus, a New World.

The discoverers and conquerors — the *conquistadores* — of the Iberian New World were natural offshoots of the seven centuries of crusading militarism against the Moors.

They were also protagonists of the rise of the Spanish middle class, the *homines novi*, or new men, of a new urban civilization slowly evolving towards local democracy, local political assemblies, charters of local rights and independent judicial authorities.

They were men who had inherited nothing: Pizarro, the conqueror of Peru, was an illiterate swine-herd; Cortés, the conqueror of Mexico, was a drop-out from law school at Salamanca University, the son of a mill owner in Estremadura: a man who had to make himself and his world.

The conquest of the New World pitted autocratic, vertically structured Indian empires against bands of Machiavellian, non-hereditary princes: princes without royal blood, princes with no pedigree except their energy, their will and their personalities.

They outwitted societies that could only hear the voices of the Gods.

The *conquistadores* heard the voices of men and women.

In Mexico, the conquest was successful because Cortés heard the complaints of the tribes subjected to the Aztecs and organized them against the supreme Indian ruler, Moctezuma.

Moctezuma heard only the voices of the Gods, and these told him that Cortés was the God Quetzalcoatl, come back to reclaim his kingdom.

Renaissance secular energy defeated a sacred, mythical world.

But the authoritarian, vertical structures of Indian power were not succeeded by horizontal, democratic structures.

They were finally replaced by another authoritarian, vertical structure, that of the Spanish Empire, as, under the king Charles V, it came to see itself as the heir to the mediaeval Holy Roman Empire.

The seeds of local democracy in Spain were crushed by Charles V when he defeated the revolution of the Castilian communities in 1521, asserting royal authority against both the weak remnants of weak Spanish feudalism and the strong currents of middle-class, urban, professional and artisanal democracy surging in the cities of Castille.

So we have this immediate irony in the very birth of Latin America: the *conquistador*, thinking he has triumphed in the New World, has just been defeated in the Old World.

Mexico City surrenders to Cortés in 1521. That same year, the chieftains of the *comunero* rebellion are executed in Castille.

When, a year ago, the municipal reforms on Mexico were introduced by the de la Madrid administration, giving municipalities, for the first time, a constitutional right to collect their own taxes and exercise their own police authority, I was shocked to realize that these basic democratic tenets came so late to us.

Why, I asked a prominent political friend in Mexico.

And he answered me: Because Charles V hung the leaders of the comunero revolution by their necks in 1521.

Was there any realistic chance for a grass-roots democracy to take hold in Latin America in the early sixteenth century?

One fact must first be understood:

Spanish feudalism was probably the weakest in Europe, for the simple reason that, starting in 711 and ending in 1492, the war of the Reconquista against the Moors meant a constant shifting of frontiers and a constant impossibility to lay claim to the land, as well as the abundance of many twilight zones and buffer regions between Christianity and Islam.

The relationship between the Crown and the explorers and conquerors is one of the great conflicts of the New World, and it defined the nature of political power in Latin America.

But the conflict also has to do with the appropriation of land and labour: it continues to be relevant if only for this powerful reason.

Who owns the wealth of Latin America?

How and to whom is it distributed?

This battle is still being waged, from Mexico and Cuba to Chile and Argentina.

But in the sixteenth century it was focussed on whether the Spanish Crown, which had just affirmed its centralist powers against a weak feudality and a vigorous democracy, was about to permit a rebirth of either factor — feudalism or democracy — in the New World.

The *conquistadores* soon simplified the political choices of the Crown.

They were products of modern-oriented individualism: they were *arrivistes*, Renaissance men on the make.

They could have chosen, as the *homines novi* of England and France did later in the seventeenth and eighteenth centuries, to stake their claims to personal ambition and social ascension on a constitutional order.

Having conquered the Indians, they would have then conquered the Crown. They would have been, as the settlers of New England were to become, the fathers of their own local democracy.

The *conquistadores* did not — perhaps they could not — choose this avenue. Between individualism as democracy and individualism as feudal might, they chose the latter.

They thus sacrificed their individualistic virtue, their Machiavellian virtu, to a spectral vision of the power their ancestors had never had.

But they must be understood: They had conquered the New World; they were the only power; they could usurp land and labour at will: Who was to stop them?

This pre-emptive possession of the wealth of the Indies always admitted the dues to the Crown: the so-called "Royal Fifth," and the *pro-forma* declaration that lands and labour were conquered in the name of the king.

But as a matter of fact, the *conquistadores* got a head start on the Crown. Both parties knew this. It was a matter of time before the conflict became acute.

When it did, the *conquistadores* facilitated the choice of the Crown.

They had not created civic, democratic communities, town halls and municipal freedoms. They wanted to be what their fathers had never been in the Old World:

They wanted to be feudal lords, *hidalgos*. The chronicler Bernal Díaz del Castillo describes Cortés, the conqueror of Mexico, preparing his expedition. As soon as he is appointed general, he begins "to adorn and to take much more care of his appearance than before." He wears "a hat of feathers, with a medallion and a gold chain, and a velvet cloak trimmed with loops of gold." Yet this splendid *hidalgo*, says Bernal, has "nothing with which to meet these expenses, for at that time he was very poor and in debt."

The spend-thrift generosity of the patrimonialist clans of Latin America and their seigneurial ambition are already depicted, by Bernal Díaz in descriptions of the figure of Cortés and the *conquistadores*.

They wanted to be *hidalgos*; they wanted to be feudal lords. And this is what the Crown set out to demolish.

Certainly, it would have also opposed a democratic direction in the settlers' politics in the New World.

Would that have posed a more difficult conundrum for Madrid? Since it did not happen we can only speculate.

The fact is that the conquerors wanted *hidalguía*, the status of gentlemen.

But *hidalguía* does not mean hard work. Quite the contrary: it means not having to labour with your hands; it means winning glory in the field of battle and then receiving the reward for your effort in lives and lands that should work for you.

The same thing happened after the Wars of Independence against Spain in the 1820s: Simón Bolívar and the other *libertadores* — much like the *conquistadores* three centuries before them — had to reward their armies, from generals to privates, with land.

The privates could not uphold their claims.

The officers could and did.

But if the armies of Independence ended by overrunning the power of the state and abusing it to this very day from Guatemala to Chile, the armies of the conquest were halted in their political and economic momentum by the Crown of Spain.

The malice and deftness with which the Spanish Crown dealt with the *conquistadores* of the New World is a case history of political expertise and one-upmanship:

These men had to be rewarded.

But not too much.

And their titles to land and labour had to remain, uncertain, precarious, revertible to the Crown after a generation or two.

The Crown unleashed on the *conquistadores* the propagandist fury of Friar Bartolomé de las Casas, ostensibly to protect the Indians from servitude but actually to protect the Crown from feudalism.

The culmination of Father de las Casas's long campaign against colonial servitude was the Laws of Indies of 1542, which proclaimed the Indians to be proprietors of the lands of the New World, while the settlers held only temporary concessions to them.

The violations of this statute are so numerous and evident that any modern auditor can not only spot them but quickly arrive at the conclusion that Latin America was founded on a dizzying contradiction between law and practice, which in effect established from the very beginning a divorce between the *real* country and the *legal* country.

The distinction is that of the French right-wing ideologue Charles Maurras: it perfectly expresses the constantly contradictory and extremely dualistic nature of Latin American societies.

Along with Father de las Casas, a dark cloud of Spanish bureaucrats, dressed in black and armed with quill pens, descended on the hapless *conquistadores* and soon reduced them to pitiful powerlessness.

Who could stand against this bevy of lawyers, councillors, inspectors, sophists and zealous representatives of political centralization?

Columbus is shipped back to Spain in irons.

Gonzolo Pizarro is publicly beheaded in Peru.

Hernán Cortés ends his life writing letters to King Charles, pathetic letters in which the conqueror depicts himself as old and poor, his properties pawned, his servants suing him for salaries due and his tailors presenting old debts.

At sixty-three, Cortés writes to the emperor, after having conquered for him a nation nine times the size of Spain, that he does not want to prowl around the Spanish inns any more, but wishes "to receive the fruit of my labours and to return to Mexico as soon as justice is done to me."

So ended these extraordinary men of the Renaissance.

But if the discovery and conquest of the New World was a feat of the Renaissance imagination, it was so because the Old World needed a Utopia and found it in the New World.

America was not discovered, says the Mexican historian Edmundo O'Gorman, it was invented.

It was needed: the excessive flow of Renaissance energies, the dramatic contradiction between its dreams of human greatness and its realities of human cruelty expressed in war, greed and apostasy, claimed for Europe a space of Utopia, a world where Europe could cleanse itself of its vices.

Saint Thomas More's *Utopia* came to the New World and was implemented in many Indian communities, from Mexico to Paraguay, by civilized friars who saw in Utopia the model needed to save the Indians from despair.

The old aboriginal worlds had come crashing down.

However shaky the position of the *conquistadores* was in the New World, they exploited Indian labour to a degree that amounted to genocide:

> The native population of the Caribbean was destroyed and had to be replaced by black slave labour imported from Africa.
>
> Between 1492 and 1640 the population of Mexico and the Antilles fell from twenty-five million to one million, and that of Andean South America from three and a half million to five hundred thousand.
>
> Slave labour in the plantation was only slightly better than slave labour in the mines.
>
> The Laws of Indies were not applied and the sharp divisions between the real country and the legal country were sharpened even more by the cynicism of the Latin American remark:
>
> *La ley se obedece, pero no se cumple*: "The law is obeyed, but then it is disregarded."

Spanish America saw the Utopian dream of its conception whipped to death on the *haciendas* of Mexico and the *encomiendas* of Cuba: Utopia disappeared down the mine shafts of Guanajuato and Potosí.

But the Crown and the Church, politically triumphant over the *conquistadores*, were not able to contain local injustices: the Crown was too far away, the Church too compromised in the double mission of evangelizing heathens and accumulating its own wealth.

The triumph of the Reformation in Europe strengthened Spain's mission as the defender of the Faith and the upholder of the repressive tenets of the counter-reformation.

The culture of Latin America arises as a response to this set of circumstances:

It was, from the very beginning, as the Cuban writer José Lezama Lima called it, "the culture of the Counter Conquest": a syncretic culture in which the naked sacrality of the Indian world could hide itself and reincarnate fully dressed in the robes of Christianity; in which African sorcerers could reappear as Catholic priests; in which idols could hide behind altars; and the huge vacuum between the dream of Utopia and the reality of colonialism could be filled — in poetry, in architecture, in religion, in food, in manners, in taste — by the expansive hunger of the Latin American baroque:

> The baroque of the magnificent poetry of the seventeenth-century Mexican nun Sor Juana Inés de la Cruz, silenced at age forty by the Church;
>
> The baroque of the magnificent statues of the eighteenth-century Brazilian sculptor Aleijadinho, creatures of a baroque, circular world demanding to be seen totally, in time as well as space.

The simplest baroque, of churches decorated following Christian gravures of the saints, but actually transforming this new religious space into Indian paradises, overflowing with the fruits of the tropics and with the smiling faces of brown Indian angels. The dramatic baroque of the bloody Christs lying dead in their glass cases, crowned with thorns, wrapped in red velvet and gold braid: a God sacrificed for men, the triumph of Christianity in an Indian culture accustomed to men being sacrificed to the Gods.

The colonial period ruined the Utopian promise of the New World.

The cities of the sun perished in the flames of robust Christian faith.

The Golden Age was melted down and sent as bullion to Spain, through whose hot and mendicant hands it slipped and went on to finance capitalist development in London, Antwerp, Hamburg and the other Northern cities to which the Jewish bourgeoisie, expelled from Spain in 1492, had migrated.

Deprived of her Jewish and Arab bankers, administrators, ministers, ambassadors, tax collectors and money lenders, Spain generated an incompetent legal bureaucracy, formal heir to the Roman tradition of the written law and imperial legitimation. Its incompetence was ably disguised by its infinite capacity for intrigue.

The failure of the so-called Invincible Armada sent by Philip II against Elizabeth I demonstrated Spain's incapacity to play a dominant role in world, or even European, affairs.

Yet at the same time its decadence began, Spain spawned one of the most brilliant constellations of writers and artists the world has known: Cervantes, Quevedo, Góngora, Velázquez, Calderón de la Barca, Saint Theresa, Saint John of the Cross, Murillo, El Greco.

The children of Iberia in the New World would also share with her this ability to compensate for the failure of history with the triumphs of art.

But Spanish America was deprived of everything modern Europe came to represent:

Religious nonconformity and civil disobedience.

Free inquiry, doubt and criticism.

The foundations of modern science and modern politics.

Spanish America was saddled with all the things European modernity judged intolerable:

Privilege as the norm; charity as the exception.

The militant Church, dogma and inquisition.

The distance between the law and its practice, between the government and the governed.

The distance between Utopian ideals and colonial realities.

The distance between the Golden Age and the Age of Iron, between the noble savage and the chained peon.

The distance between the law and its practice, between the Crown and its colonies and between the social layers and institutions of the colonies themselves.

Between the isolated localities and the central metropolis.

Between the old and the new Gods.

Between the real country and the legal country.

Between the spiritual mission and the temporal wealth of the Church.

Between the two nations: haves and have-nots.

Between expectations and rewards.

This distance set the stage, by the end of the eighteenth century, for national independence in the former colonies of Spain and Portugal in the New World.

It also charged us with changing these realities by ourselves, since they are a part of our centuries-old experience.

Their persistence is a challenge to us today.

Our family quarrels have their origins in them.

We are, because of our tradition, at war with ourselves.

And only we can truly understand and solve these problems.

III

ON Palm Sunday 1766, angry mobs attacked the residence of the Marquis di Squillace, a minister in the court of the Bourbon king of Spain, Charles III.

The marquis, who was Italian by birth, was judged guilty of violating a decree forbidding big floppy hats and flowing dark capes in Madrid, because they helped criminals to strike and escape unknown. Instead, *madrileños* were encouraged to wear the three-cornered hat, which made them indisguisable.

This assault on Madrid's proverbial sense of drama, which perhaps hit lovers harder than criminals, was part of King Charles's modernization campaign, which pretended to propel Spain out of the long Hapsburg lethargy that began with the defeat of the Invincible Armada and ended with the childless reign of Charles II — Charles the Bewitched, the impotent, retarded monarch who cured his splitting headaches by having pigeons killed on top of his head and feeling the warm blood drip down his face.

The treasures of the New World slipped through the fingers of the Hapsburg monarchy and went abroad to pay for costly wars, imported manufactures and grandiose conceits such as Philip II's imperial monastery and necropolis at El Escorial, the place, the poet García Lorca would write, where all the cold rains in the world come from.

The distant American colonies of Spain were colonies of a colony. For if we became the colony of Spain, Spain became a colony of northern, capitalist Europe.

We were the Indies of Spain.

Spain was the Indies of Europe.

Louis XIV of France put it most succinctly: "Let us now sell merchandise to the Spanish and obtain from them gold and silver."

Hapsburg disorganization distanced the colonies from Madrid: the very laxness of imperial authority during the long decline of the seventeenth century furthered the movement towards some kind of self-reliance in the American colonies.

These were rapidly becoming Creole nations; that is, nations dominated by the white descendants of Spaniards in the New World. But the Creoles — the *criollos* — were certainly not the majority in Spanish America.

By 1810, when the revolutions of independence, with astonishing simultaneity, caught fire from the vice-royalty of New Spain — Mexico — in the North to the vice-royalty of the River Plate — Buenos Aires — in the South, Creoles constituted roughly nineteen percent of the twenty-three million inhabitants of Iberian America. Indians were thirty-six percent and blacks, mulattos and mestizos forty-five percent.

But the Creoles, more and more, came to control land and labour, and, left to themselves and their wiles, they even started minimal programmes of manufacturing and commercial expansion based on the abundance of raw material and cheap labour.

Now, the reforms introduced by Charles III in Spain meant modernization of Spain but they also meant further colonization of the colonies to pay for Spanish modernization.

The colonies were told that they would be more than ever dependent on the metropolis: denied the right to manufacture and forced to import manufactured goods from Spain; denied the right to trade among themselves and obliged to trade only with the metropolis.

The monarchy's response to the Squillace riots had been to blame them on the Jesuits and expel the Company of Jesus from Spain and her colonies in 1767.

The Jesuits had been introducing the study of science, mathematics, geography and history into the colonies, dominated until then by scholastic thinking and Inquisitorial supervision.

Books were smuggled in: Voltaire, Rousseau, Montesquieu.

News arrived: revolution in France, revolution in the thirteen American colonies of Britain.

Questions were raised:

Could one substitute a monarchy with a republic?

Could one oust a colonial power?

Why were the French and Spanish monarchies supporting the claims of the rebels in Virginia, the anti-monarchists in Massachusetts, the republicans in Pennsylvania?

Could we also become modern nations?

Could we also become independent nations?

These questions radicalized the intellectuals of the colonies.

They radicalized the lower clergy, whose privileges were taken away from them by the modernizing zeal of the Bourbons.

They radicalized the local militia, who, for the first time, had a taste of victory in Buenos Aires in 1806, when they defeated a British invasion that the vice-roy had been incapable of repelling.

They radicalized the Creole merchants, who spoke through the voice of Manuel Moreno in Argentina, demanding freedom to import what they did not have and freedom to export what was left over to pay for it.

They radicalized the mestizos, the Latin Americans of mixed European and Indian descent, who in 1781 marched on Bogotá demanding more opportunities for Americans and better treatment for Indians.

They radicalized the expelled Jesuits, who identified with the cause of Americanism and wrote national histories of Mexico and Chile from Rome, where they intrigued against the Spanish monarchy.

All of these factors came to a boil in 1808, when, for the first time since the invasion of the Moors, Spain was occupied by a foreign power, Napoleonic France, which deposed the Bourbon monarch, Ferdinand VII.

The colonies immediately declared that, in the absence of a Spanish king, they were free to govern themselves until the monarchy was restored in Madrid.

When that happened, it was too late:

The momentum of the Independence extended from Mexico City to Buenos Aires.

And as the Creoles with their mestizo, black and Indian armies fought the Spanish royalists during the next fifteen years, all the past contradictions — and a set of new ones — made their appearance in Latin America:
While retaining the traumatic events of:
conquest and colonization;
a lost Utopia;
a reverberating aboriginal myth;
and a desperate baroque and syncretic culture,
Latin America now heaped conflict upon conflict:
Independence revealed the existence within each polity of two nations;
It not only revealed it but furthered it:
Most attempts to bridge the gulf between haves and have-nots were merely legalistic and in themselves furthered a second conflict, the colonial conflict between the legal country and the real country:
The Indians everywhere were given full civil liberties and equality by the insurgents.
But they remained the victims of serfdom and economic backwardness.

The Spanish past was brutally denied.
In its place, we set the shining examples of Britain, France and the United States.
By emulating them, by copying their laws, we would instantly become like them: modern, progressive, prosperous, democratic.

This was not to be, and the tremendous gulf between law and reality, between desire and its object, was filled by the *caudillo*, the Machiavellian strong man, the dictatorial figure capable of maintaining a semblance of unity in the pulverized societies that followed independence:

from Juan Manuel de Rosas in Argentina

to Porfirio Díaz in Mexico;

passing through the sinister Doctor Francia, who shut Paraguay off from the world;

or the tragicomic Santa Anna, who lost half of Mexico to the United States;

or the wily Juan Vicente Gómez, who opened up Venezuela to the petroleum companies.

These figures perpetuated the colonial situation of the majority while, at best, creating prosperity for the minority.

Simón Bolívar, the Liberator, had attempted to bridge these realities of real and legal country, of prosperous minorities and dispossessed minorities, of central and local authority, through what, in effect, was the model for compromise between two forms of Latin American conservatism: national and regional.

At best, this furthered an inauthentic progress, in which Latin America profited from the world-wide expansion of capitalism by providing it with raw materials but without providing ourselves with capital for investment and savings.

In the nineteenth century, we became orphans of our own peripheral capitalism, feverishly substituting imports to uphold patterns of consumption in the middle to upper classes, while again postponing any rational approach to the welfare of the majority.

Since Independence, we had been practising our version of Cactus Reaganomics:

Let the rich grow richer and eventually the poor will become less poor.

From his deathbed in Santa Marta in 1830, Simón Bolívar wrote in disillusionment and despair:

"America is ungovernable. Those who serve the revolution plough the seas."

This is quite moving and perhaps even melodramatic, but in reality there were things to be done then, as there are things to be done today, in Latin America.

We can try to understand all the negative factors of our history:

the weight of Indian autocracy and Spanish imperialism;

colonial structures;

legal legerdemain and economic injustice.

But there is no determinism in all of this.

We made our own history and we can change it:

Real country against legal country.

Central against local authority.

Two nations.

The army as arbiter of power.

Economies oriented towards serving the few by increasing foreign dependency.

All this is true, if not good, but nothing says it is eternal.

The revolutions of independence left a profound residue of nationalism in our countries.

It can be argued that this only further divided us.

It can also be argued that, thanks to it, we have been able to sustain a minimal identity, which has furthered the continuity of our culture and helped us to defend ourselves from foreign pressures.

The continuity of our culture:

From the epic poet of the conquest of Chile, Alonso de Ercilla, to the modern poet of the reconquest of Spanish America, Pablo Neruda;

From the baroque statuary of the colonial sculptor of Brazil, Aleijadinho, to the cosmic figures of the modern Mexican painter, Rufino Tamayo;

From the mythic oral traditions of the jungle and the mountain to the modern narrative myths of Gabriel García Márquez;

Latin American culture has maintained an uninterrupted vitality.

This continuity is in brutal contrast to the hesitations and failures of our political history.

Yet through the unity of civilization and the Balkanization of politics, we are challenged to create a model of progress of our own; not an extra-logical imitation of Western forms, but a critical model of our own, pertaining to our own culture, European, Indian, black, mestizo, born of our needs and experiences.

This model has attempted to express itself through nationalism and through revolution: extreme forms of historical assertion and historical violence that, in order to change our societies without sacrificing their deeper unity, must meet the demands of cultural creation.

Independent Latin America was to suffer grievously from foreign intervention and even dismemberment, as well as from foreign economic imperialism.

Both our strengths and weaknesses as a culture and as independent nations soon came into conflict with another revolutionary force of the times: the United States of America.

The admiration of the American Revolution had been enormous in Latin America, as great as the admiration of the French Revolution. Even more so, perhaps, as Washington and his men were, like us, Americans, former colonials, who proved capable of inaugurating a strong, vital democracy: of creating a New Nation.

This admiration was expressed through the widespread reproduction of the tenets of the Constitution of the United States in the new Latin American republics. But this, yet another example of what the French sociologist Jean-Gabriel de Tarde called "extra-logical imitation," only reinforced the Latin American duality of a legal country disguising a real country.

Furthermore, attitudes towards the United States soon aligned themselves on partisan lines, and these had a lot to do with the acceptance or refusal of the past.

The two main political parties in nineteenth-century Latin America were Conservatives and Liberals.

The Conservatives did not want a revolutionary, progressive future, but a reactionary past, in which the aristocracy and the Church retained their privileges.

They also feared and hated the United States:

Because the new republic signified modern values — indeed, modernity at any price, and the sacrifice of tradition;

Because it meant Protestantism versus Catholicism;

Because it meant revolutionary populism versus monarchical authority;

Because it meant progressive capitalism versus semi-feudal stagnation;

Because it meant their strength against our weakness, and strength as expansionism.

The Liberals, on the contrary, were the pro-Americans, who hailed in the United States all that the Conservatives decried.

Yet Liberal admiration for the United States was soon to meet Conservative suspicion as the former

Thirteen Colonies asserted themselves, and their imperial ambitions in this hemisphere became manifest — became, indeed, Manifest Destiny:

As early as 1801, President Thomas Jefferson was writing to James Monroe:

> "However our present interests may restrain us within our own limits, it is impossible not to look forward to distant times when our rapid multiplication will expand itself beyond those limits, and cover the whole northern, if not the southern continent, with a people speaking the same language, governed in a similar form, and by similar laws."

These sweeping exclusions of the cultural differences that might conceivably exist between a homogeneous, metropolitan United States and a heterogeneous, eccentric Latin America were not accepted by Henry Clay when he responded to similar assertions of manifest destiny from John Quincy Adams in 1821:

> "Will gentlemen contend, because those people are not like us in all particulars, they are therefore unfit for freedom?"

But Adams answers Clay and persists: it is "unavoidable that the remainder of the continent should be ours."

Latin America did not have to wait for Jefferson's "distant times" before it was partially taken over: President Polk's war against Mexico in 1847 and the dismemberment of the independent republic, then the takeover of Nicaragua in 1857 by the American free-booter William Walker, and finally the declaration by President Cleveland's secretary of state, Richard Olney, in 1895, that "today the United States is practically sovereign on this continent, and its fiat is law upon the subjects to which it confines its interposition," convinced even liberal admirers of United States democracy that the democracy was also an empire and that this was its strength, but perhaps, also, its weakness.

The shadow of the United States was a primordial factor in the assertion of a Latin American political, diplomatic and cultural identity since the nineteenth century.

Whenever Latin America has moved to deal radically with its conflictive heritage, it has clashed with the incapacity of the United States to come to terms with four intimately interrelated issues: Nationalism and Change, Redistribution of power and Negotiations.

This is the challenge, and Anthony Lewis has best stated it, recently, in the *New York Times*:

> "There is going to be social change in the Third World. The United States should learn to live with such change, even promote it, instead of treating every challenge to the status quo as Soviet inspired, requiring East-West confrontation."

This is now truer than ever in the present-day conflict surrounding events in Central America and the Caribbean.

We shall deal with this situation in the next two lectures, but before we do so, it is important to understand that Latin America, its difficult past, its problems unsolved, its problems yet to come, can only be taken care of by Latin Americans.

Our debate is a debate within, a debate with ourselves, a family quarrel. The interference of extraneous factors only postpones our solutions and corrupts our legitimate aspirations.

As our terrible century comes to an end, we clearly perceive that everywhere ideologies die and cultures reappear as the true harbingers of a more complete and conscious way of life.

Perhaps Latin America will come to know its real identity in this flowering, as the millennium ends, of the hidden faces of civilizations.

Latin America is part of a world-wide movement towards pluralism in international relations and a push away from bi-polar relations.

The arrogant nostalgia of both world powers over their so-called "spheres of influence" is the cause of a vacuum first and an escalation later, endangering both change and national independence in Latin America.

Sometimes, we think that the real menace to each of the great powers is not the other power, but the independence of the national states: Poland or Nicaragua, El Salvador or Afghanistan, Honduras or Czechoslovakia.

We must overcome this sterile dualism in order to know our place in the new concert of cultures that seems to prefigure the physiognomy of the coming century.

In such a concert, perhaps Latin America shall discover that it has something to do, something to say, something to recover and something to give.

IV

THERE is a passage in the novel *One Hundred Years of Solitude* by Gabriel García Márquez in which the patriarch José Arcadio Buendía decides that from now on it shall always be Monday.

If a Latin American Rip Van Winkle had gone to sleep, say, in 1928, and now woke up, he would have this extraordinary sense of *déja vu*: it is always Monday in relations between the United States and Latin America.

Where are we? Why is the president of the United States denouncing Mexico — I'm sorry, Nicaragua as the source of Bolshevik subversion in Central America?

Why is Honduras occupied by United States Marines?

Why are warships in Caribbean waters demonstrating that diplomacy comes from the mouth of a cannon?

Who has decided all this?

Rip Van Winkle would answer: "President Calvin Coolidge. This is 1928. This is Monday, so it must be Nicaragua."

We would have to exclaim, in despair, "There we go again!" as the perennial question of our relations with the United States is posed once more, as if nothing had happened between 1928 and 1984:

Can the United States learn to live with revolutionary movements in the Western hemisphere? But also, can revolutionary movements in the Western hemisphere live with the United States?

Spokesmen of the present administration in Washington answer affirmatively: Yes, of course. We have nothing against revolutions, as long as they remain indigenous, democratic and independent of the Soviet Union. If they are kidnapped, if they become undemocratic, if, indeed, they become too closely allied to the Soviet bloc, then, in the name of both democracy and self-interest, we must oppose them.

The problem with this answer is that it is totally ahistorical, not to say hypocritical.

No revolution in this hemisphere has come to power with a more decisive quota of extra-continental backing than the American Revolution.

Not only was Lafayette here, so were de Grasse and his fleets, Rochambeau and his regiments.

But the fact that the revolution was supported from abroad did not transform the Founding Fathers into agents of the Bourbon monarchy of France.

The fact that the American Revolution was imperfect, marred by slavery and deep social inequalities, would not have justified a counter-revolution organized by a foreign power invoking *un*democratic aspects of American life.

Indeed, many American Tories "voted with their feet," as they say today, and left in waves — up to a hundred thousand people out of a population of two and a half million — to more amiable, pro-British shores.

The American contras and their sponsors were finally defeated, once and for all, in the War of 1812, even if boundaries and other contentious issues with England were not solved, by slow diplomatic means, until 1840.

The point is that revolutions, in the first place, are unique.

They are born from concrete local circumstances and nothing on earth can create them artificially.

It was not Louis XVI who imposed revolution on the Thirteen Colonies, and it is not the Soviet Union who can impose revolution on Latin America.

This would be tantamount to saying, as the Soviets say, that the Solidarity movement in Poland is a creature of the CIA.

What the Soviet Union can do in Central America — or the United States in Central Europe — is to profit marginally from the mistakes of the other great power in its traditional sphere of influence.

Thus, the question is to avoid these mistakes, not to compound them.

Revolutions cannot be imported or exported: they are not bananas.

Only the movements in Mexico, Cuba, Nicaragua and now El Salvador can be called violent revolutions in Latin America in this century.

The radical transformations in Guatemala in the forties and fifties, and in Chile in the sixties and seventies, were initiated by popularly elected governments.

Other important changes have been made by non-radical, evolutionary governments in Costa Rica, the Dominican Republic and Venezuela.

This means that armed revolutions or radical politics are not the only way, of course; and, in any case, they seem to be exceptional.

Movements without a true indigenous base fail, out of their own artificiality: this is what happened to Che

Guevara in Bolivia and to the guerrilla bands in Venezuela in the early sixties.

Furthermore, some countries, such as Chile and Argentina, have a sufficient foundation in the development of civil society to return to it when they have overthrown a military dictatorship.

Others, such as El Salvador and Nicaragua, face the fact that they lack any institutional, problem-saving structure worthy of the name, and that revolutions are a way of creating institutions where you have none.

This is the cultural and historical reality that the current sophism on the choice between gentle authoritarianism or hideous totalitarianism will not understand.

So the fuss is about historical situations that are unique, rare, indigenous, not subject to export or import, but are invariably seen as profoundly offensive, even dangerous, to the prestige and to the security of the United States.

I will argue that it is the traditional response of the United States to revolution, more than the revolutions themselves, that finally threatens the interests of the United States.

The Mexican Revolution of 1910 overthrew the longstanding dictatorship of Porfirio Díaz; and, after free elections in 1911, it brought to the presidency the most democratic régime we have ever had in Mexico: that of Francisco Madero.

But Madero was promptly overthrown, in 1913, by collusion between the regular army of the dictatorship, which he had failed to transform, and the ambassador of the Taft administration, Henry Lane Wilson.

Through its military and constructive phases, between 1910 and 1930, the Mexican Revolution was bitterly opposed by the United States; yet by no stretch of the imagination could it be stamped as Marxist-Leninist or pro-Soviet.

Yet President Calvin Coolidge, generally a taciturn individual, stated before a joint session of Congress in 1927 that Mexico was the source of Bolshevik subversion in central America.

Mexico's sin was to aid Sandino, the Nicaraguan rebel, as he fought off the occupation of Nicaragua by the Marines — the third occupation in the first quarter of this century.

This external sin marked another internal sin: Mexico's decision to recover the resources of its subsoil and implement agrarian reform. These internal decisions were the basis for arguments in the United States favouring foreign intervention against the Mexican Revolution.

That is why, when the United States intervenes violently in Central America, we Mexicans ask ourselves: Are we next?

And it is for these same reasons that many of us in Latin America doubt that the real problem for the United States is Marxism-Leninism, but rather that it is the assertion of national independence.

It is the national independence of the countries to the south of the United States that bothers the governments of the United States; more than ideological tags it can certainly live with, when the Marxist-Leninist régimes are called Yugoslavia or China, and when they oppose, for their own national and independent reasons, the paramount power in their own region: the Soviet Union.

The problem of spheres of influence always has the name of the dominant power that defines the nature of intervention in each sphere: the Soviet Union in Czechoslovakia; the United States in Nicaragua.

The Sandinista revolution was not fathered by the Soviet Union.

But General Wojciech Jaruzelski is kept in power by the Soviet Union.

And General Anastasio Somoza was put in power in Nicaragua by the United States.

The extremely violent revolution in Mexico, which cost more than one million human lives, learned three paramount lessons, which have also been or are being learned by other revolutionary movements in this hemisphere:

> First: The revolutions have taken hold where a revolutionary army has backed them: Mexico, Cuba and Nicaragua;
>
> Second: They have been overturned where the revolutionary army did not exist or where a traditional standing army had the capacity to overthrow the radical régime: Guatemala in 1954 and Chile in 1973. The price for these mistakes has been very high:
>
> > Thirty years of genocide, repression and economic crisis in Guatemala.
> >
> > Eleven years of genocide, repression and economic crisis in Chile.
> >
> > And a widespread conviction that democratically elected left-wing régimes incapable of defending themselves with arms are doomed, dooming with them the hope that radical reforms through the vote can be obtained in Latin America. The events in Guatemala and Chile convinced many

Latin Americans that the United States would not tolerate such an outcome. Armed insurrection was, then, the only way to reform; and

Third: The revolutions have taken hold where a popular mobilization in support of the revolution and its aims has occurred, arming the people themselves.

This raises the issue of social reforms and democratic advancement.

Great social advances are thus made, especially in health, work and education, but they are sometimes achieved at a very high price of personal and democratic freedoms.

All things being equal, there should be no contradiction between social progress and individual freedoms.

But all things are not equal.

The searing, open wound of the historical memory of Mexico is the War of 1847 with the United States and the loss of half our national territory because we were a weak and disorganized nation.

The leaders of the Mexican Revolution decided that this should not happen again: all the policies of the revolution were subsumed under a will to nationalism that made it possible to negotiate with the Americans frankly, firmly and with dignity.

Nationalism at the cost of democracy.

If the price of unpolluted democracy, such as Madero had practised, was the counter-revolutionary restoration and the supremacy of American will in Mexican affairs, then democracy would have to wait, without being renounced.

The Nation took precedence over the Democracy.

It was hoped that concrete social advancement would generate the Democracy.

Yet however tenuous the Mexican commitment to democracy, the United States has been able to live with it.

What the United States has no business doing is demanding instant democracy of the Sandinistas in Nicaragua — and never demanding it of Pinochet in Chile — while in effect having tolerated the Somoza dictatorship for forty years.

The urgency to build a nation has proved stronger than the urge to build a democracy in the eccentric reaches of the former Spanish Empire, and nothing has served this better than the tense relationship with the United States:

Carlos Franqui, the Cuban revolutionary who broke with Fidel Castro, explains in his recent book, *Family Portrait with Fidel,* how the Bay of Pigs operation and CIA intervention against Castro only strengthened the Cuban régime and permitted it to clamp down on its enemies because the CIA made most Cubans believe that to be in the opposition meant to be against Cuba and for the United States.

And also, United States activities against a revolutionary régime serve as a justification for searching for Soviet support. Alliance with the Soviet Union might appear as a national-security imperative for the besieged country.

Revolutions in Latin America should be deprived of the justifications offered by successive United States administrations to authoritarian rule of the left.

Marxism-Leninism becomes a mask for traditional authoritarianism justified by American aggression.

Remove American aggression and let us move by ourselves, without external justification, to resolve our own family quarrels: Latin America is not at war with the United States, it is at war with itself.

This is no time for historical amnesia. To forget can be disastrous.

The memory we should be holding present is that the United States can co-exist with revolutionary régimes on its frontiers and that revolutionary régimes in the Western hemisphere can co-exist with the United States.

Mexico, again, is the example of what I'm trying to convey.

By the late 1930s, Mexico reached an agreement with the United States: a *modus vivendi* was established between presidents Lázaro Cárdenas and Franklin D. Roosevelt, when the expropriation of Mexican oil, the dynamics of the "good-neighbour" policy and the imminence of World War Two made it advisable to bury the hatchet and count on Mexico as an ally that would guarantee a secure southern border for the United States.

The easing of relations with the United States meant the decline of the army as a factor in Mexican politics.

It also opened doors to trade and other relations that have transformed Mexico into the first foreign supplier of oil to the United States and into its third-largest trading partner, world-wide.

Roosevelt's legacy of mutual and pragmatic respect reached its legal maturity under the Truman administration, as the United States and Latin America arrived at substantial political and diplomatic compromises during the international conferences in Bogotá in 1948 and Quitandinha in 1949.

The American delegations, led by George Marshall, accepted the trade-off between what interested Latin America most — non-intervention — in the Charter of the OAS drafted in Bogotá, and what most interested the United States — collective security — in the Rio Treaty, the Treaty of Reciprocal Assistance.

The Roosevelt and Truman legacies were then undermined by the ascendancy of John Foster Dulles: The United States does not have friends, he declared, it has interests.

The deterioration of this legal framework ever since the CIA's intervention in Guatemala thirty years ago has now reached the point of risking being totally crushed under the weight of policies that disdain diplomacy and the law in favour of militaristic solutions that only compound and prolong conflicts they cannot contain or resolve.

The biggest difference between the United States and Latin America is simply this: They are a developed nation. We are developing nations. Our realities, our reflexes, our responses, our achievements cannot be measured with the same tape.

The United States was instantly equipped for democracy, with all its failings.

We were not, simply because the realities on which they could establish their own democratic polity were absent from the vertically ordained, autocratic orderings of both the Indian and the Iberian empires of the Americas.

The United States, with its short, nervous, puritanical, futuristic history, is impatient.

Latin America, with its long, languorous, Iberian, Aztec, Quechuan, Amazonian and baroque history, is patient.

So we must come back to the cultural connection — or the cultural divide, if you prefer — in order to answer the pervasive political question: Can the United States co-exist with revolutionary régimes in Latin America? Can revolutionary régimes in Latin America co-exist with the United States?

What comes after the triumph of a revolution?

An unsavoury Marxist-Leninist régime?

More: An unsavoury anti-American Marxist-Leninist régime?

Or a régime that calls itself Marxist-Leninist but need not be anti-American?

A régime that calls itself Marxist-Leninist in order to achieve modernist legitimation but is not culturally so, rather an offshoot of deeper Latin American traditions, Thomist, Catholic, hierarchical, dogmatic, monistic, nationalistic, anti-capitalistic because of its allegiance to the Council of Trent rather than to the politburo in Moscow?

Or even, let me add, a régime that calls itself Marxist-Leninist but cannot follow the Soviet model because diplomatic, economic and political realities make it unnecessary or unprofitable or even unthinkable for it to behave that way?

I would like to believe that a major power such as the United States, accompanied by friends and allies in this hemisphere, Europe and Asia, can find multiple, creative, positive ways to deal constructively with a newborn revolution determined to bring about quick social change and in need of a diversified and healthy relationship with the world economy.

The nature of a revolutionary régime in the Americas is decided by many factors: its own internal dynamics, including its need to assert independence from the United States and even call the United States names in order to prove it; but also the external dynamics of economic interdependence, which can be effectively attuned to diversification and mutual benefit.

Diplomacy is the bridge between:

One: The patience required in facing the revolutionary need to work historic fevers out of a nation's system, especially when that history has been based on subservience to the main regional power: Poland in Central Europe; Nicaragua in Central America;

Two: The imagination required to deal in a normal diplomatic fashion with the internal events of revolution;

And three: The interested astuteness needed to channel the released energies of a national revolution into the only available international economic structure.

As Richard Feinberg and Kenneth Oye have recently argued in *World Policy*, the United States must understand that "a nation's domestic political economy does not determine its mode of participation in the international economy."

Authoritarian or liberal politics, statism or decentralized economies, "a break occurs at the shoreline of the international economy."

Working capital; equipment; infrastructure: transport, storage, power, health, education. This, according to William H. Bolin, the former vice-president of the Bank of America, is what Central America needs and should be receiving. Political solutions, he argues, will flow from economic solutions, not vice versa.

Each country in the region, adds Bolin, must move forward on its own. It would be a tragic error for the

United States to participate in the economic programmes being pushed for Central America only after Central America arrives at political solutions to the liking of one or another political point of view in the United States.

Mr. Bolin's sensible advice has not been heeded.

Good economic money has been thrown after bad military money, nullifying both.

The EEC ministers, meeting in September in San José, the capital of Costa Rica, were pressured by Secretary of State Shultz to exclude Nicaragua from their economic projects for the region.

Should we wonder that, if Nicaragua were to be spurned economically by Europe and Japan, it should turn to the Soviet Union? No.

Instead of political, economic or diplomatic solutions, we have been offered the spectacle of the world's most powerful democracy mining harbours, refusing the jurisdiction of the World Court, publishing primers on political assassination and putting the machines of war before the steeds of diplomacy.

The problem is that the military solution is not working.

It is not working in El Salvador, where at least fifty percent of the arms used by the guerrillas are American arms, sent by the present administration to defend democracy in El Salvador, and which then turn up in the hands of the guerrillas because the demoralized army abandons them in the field or, even worse, their commanders sell them to the guerrillas, at a profit, at Ilopango Air Force Base.

Meanwhile, no one seems capable of dominating the death squads, and their actions have now surpassed malnutrition as the principal cause of death in El Salvador.

But let us rejoice. A goodly part of the sums sent by the United States as economic aid to El Salvador tends to show up in the Miami bank accounts of the Salvadoran oligarchy and army commanders: they are, shall we say, recycled dollars that come back to a secure haven in this country.

Millions are poured in. But at best a military standstill is procured. And a military stalemate finally means a rebel victory. Since this has become unacceptable to United States policy makers, since the army cannot win the civil war, and if the Salvadoran government of José Napoleón Duarte cannot control the army, only one avenue is left; and that is United States military occupation of El Salvador.

If this should occur — and it may occur in Honduras as well — the United States will discover the face and name of its true foe in Latin America: not Marxism-Leninism, but nationalism.

And when the United States collides with Third World nationalism, it faces defeat, as it did in Viet Nam. The same goes for Soviet imperialism, which must face nationalism more and more, on two fronts: Afghanistan and China in the East, and also Poland, Czechoslovakia, Romania, Hungary, East Germany and even Bulgaria in the West.

Let me express my hope here that President Duarte can deal with three major problems:

One: Dominating the military and bringing the death squads to justice;

Two: Defusing regional tensions by co-operating with Nicaragua in the application of the Contadora Act, which forbids both countries from aiding insurgency in the other or from accepting foreign bases or foreign military trainers on their soil;

Three: Establishing a form of political dialogue with the opposition, which now cannot participate in the national debate or in national elections without danger of being assassinated by the death squads.

After all, President Duarte, back in 1972, won the election heading a ticket on which he ran for president and the present head of the insurrected opposition, Guillermo Ungo, ran for vice-president.

Perhaps President Duarte's dramatic initiative at La Palma recently will help recreate the centre-left solution in El Salvador once more.

Diplomacy will further the chances of such a solution.

Military interventionism will nullify them.

There are no façile military solutions in Central America.

The invasion of Nicaragua by the only force capable of toppling the Sandinistas — the armed force of the United States — would not be a swift pre-emptive operation as in Grenada:

> The Sandinistas are perfectly prepared to take up the armed resistance they left but six years ago.
>
> The *contras* would be given power.
>
> They would stage a blood-bath and restore the essential Somoza dictatorship that served the United States without a murmur for forty years.

One of the most violent civil wars this hemisphere has known would ensue, with the United States caught right in the middle of it:

Occupy El Salvador and Honduras.

Invade Nicaragua.

Proclaim a generalized war against Communism in Central America.

Destabilize Mexico through arm-twisting policies determined by a right-wing cabbala in Washington.

Bring the war to the southern frontier of the United States.

Inflate the Central American soufflé to the bursting point and postpone co-operation on the solution of the really big problems.

This would surely be the culmination of the self-fulfilling domino prophecy.

This is, if ever there was one, a recipe for disaster.

It must be avoided.

It can be avoided, through the most honourable and positive means: negotiations.

This is what will take care of the security, the credibility and the prestige of the United States.

And of the lives of the young men of America.

V

TWO clear possibilities still stand in Central America. One is called diplomacy. The other is called war.

No one asks a major power to renounce the use of force as a legitimate and ultimate instance of persuasion. What many of us criticize is the use of force not as an ultimate but as an initial instrument of persuasion, in present United States policies in Central America.

Pro-forma support is given to diplomatic negotiations; but this always finally turns out to be lip service.

The Contadora Act on Peace and Co-operation in Central America, after a long and patient process of negotiation carried out by Mexico, Colombia, Panama and Venezuela in the face of enormous political and military difficulties, has now been approved by all five concerned republics: Guatemala, El Salvador, Honduras, Costa Rica and Nicaragua.

This diplomatic instrument halts the introduction of new arms systems that would "modify qualitatively or quantitatively" the present arms balance in the region.

It eliminates foreign military bases and training centres.

It establishes a timetable for withdrawing all foreign military advisers.

It eliminates "regional and extra-regional arms traffic to persons, organizations, irregular forces or armed bands that are trying to destabilize governments."

It eliminates, in effect, any conceivable danger to United States security interests; in effect, outlaws a Soviet military presence in the region; and, in effect, opens the door to long-range political, economic and social solutions.

The United States and Nicaragua, meeting seriously at the Mexican port of Manzanillo since June 1984, have been able to dissipate the smoke and heat of rhetoric and reach what seemed to be substantial agreements.

One of them was that the Nicaraguan régime would sign the Contadora Act, thus demonstrating its good faith in achieving peace in Central America.

But when Nicaragua, in agreement, it would seem, with the United States, signs the Contadora Act, the United States denounces Nicaragua for employing public-relations ploys and refuses to go along with the peace plan, thus confusing everyone, starting with the other Central American republics and then the friends of the United States in the region, especially the four Contadora nations, which have worked so hard at finding this solution and then have seen it boycotted at the last minute by the country that, rationally, should most benefit from it: the United States.

There should be no obstacles.

But there seems to be an enormous one, and it is this: Negotiations bind all parties.

Not only Nicaragua or Cuba or the Soviet Union.

They also bind the United States.

We have to conclude, in sadness, at the latest reading, that it is not Nicaragua's capacity for subverting anyone, nor its arms buildup, nor the possibility of its offering the Russians bases and military allegiance — since these are all dangers that the Contadora Act eliminates — but Nicaragua's independence from Washington that Washington does not like:

The interruption of a secular arrangement by which a small and weak Central American state must behave as a protectorate of the major continental power or go the way of the Lithuanias and the Polands of this world.

The United States cannot roll over and disappear from the scene.

Because of its weight, it cannot practise non-non-intervention in the Americas.

But neither should it practise negative intervention, as it has traditionally done, with the bright exception of the Roosevelt era.

It should practise the politics of positive non-intervention.

These are the politics of normalcy.

The United States should be a civilized presence in this hemisphere, dedicated to dealing with problems, not ignoring or exacerbating them.

It should be respectful of everyone's internal politics and realities: Cuba or Chile, Nicaragua or Mexico, Argentina or Honduras.

It should consider that its strength lies in respect for the rule of law.

It should consider that its advantages are called democracy, humane political traditions, world-wide economic links and strong and respectful relationships with its allies, its trading partners and its neighbours.

Are these not bases of strength from which to negotiate the present contentious issues directly with Cuba or Nicaragua?

Strengthen the United States by dealing diplomatically with Cuba, Nicaragua and the Contadora countries.

Do not strengthen the Soviet Union by ignoring or threatening these countries.

Are these not bases of strength for an accommodation to what Abraham Lowenthal calls "hegemony lost" in this hemisphere?

"No United States administration to date," writes Lowenthal, "has dealt successfully with the decline of United States hegemony and its implications, nor with the consequences of Latin America's social and economic transformation."

This transformation has now spoken clearly through the Contadora process.

The United States is being served notice that Latin America can negotiate its own diplomatic solutions.

Central America has signalled that it can rule itself if left to itself.

The Contadora Act has become a Latin American Declaration of Independence.

We have taken responsibility for our future.

The United States now tells us that this is intolerable:

That Latin America shall only be what the administration in Washington wants it to be;

That diplomatic negotiations are to be treated with smiling condescension while they are in progress;

But that diplomatic negotiations are not to be respected once they are agreed upon, especially if the agreements are reached without United States' approval.

At that moment, the United States pressures some of the weaker nations in Central America in order to sabotage openly the peace process.

The Contadora Act sets a new litmus test for all of us, from Mexico to Argentina:

The United States must not only learn to negotiate with Latin America;

It must also learn to respect negotiations freely arrived at by Latin Americans without the United States.

For God's sake, if the United States are incapable of themselves negotiating, at least let us negotiate with ourselves.

The most constructive attitude the president of the United States could take is to meet immediately with the presidents of the four Contadora nations and to put the weight of the United States behind the peace process.

The Contadora Act was not drawn up by Nicaragua or by the Soviet Union, but by four proven friends of the United States: Mexico, Panama, Colombia and Venezuela.

It is not the result of a Communist conspiracy but of the diplomatic imagination and political will of presidents de la Madrid, Ardito Barletta, Betancur and Lusinchi.

If the United States cannot deal with them, who can they deal with in this hemisphere?

Does the United States want friends, or does it want satellites?

Since the end of World War Two, the planet has been dominated by bi-polarism: the dual hegemony of the United States and the Soviet Union.

Bi-polarism implies the arrogant pretension of carving out "spheres of influence" for each great power.

This, in turn, belies the principles of non-intervention and self-determination and promotes coercion, force and political or economic intervention in the affairs of countries within each so-called "sphere of influence": Poland or Nicaragua, Afghanistan or El Salvador.

The Monroe Doctrine, in 1823, was one of the first manifestations of what eventually became contemporary bi-polarism, a unilateral declaration about who could and could not make himself present in this hemisphere, without consulting the Latin American republics and in effect tying them as much as possible to the will and the destiny — the manifest destiny — of the United States.

The practice of tsarism in Europe and Asia did not need a comparable doctrine: it asserted itself, if possible, on the eastern and southern and western boundaries of the Russian Empire.

The Brezhnev Doctrine, in 1968, justified the invasion of Czechoslovakia by the Warsaw Pact forces on the grounds that, once in the Soviet sphere, you stay in the Soviet sphere.

But Alexander Dubček, the leader of the Prague Spring, was not planning to leave the Soviet alliance: he was presiding over a truly socialist movement in a nominally socialist country, where socialism was in effect forbidden. This was the real danger to Moscow.

The reverse Brezhnev Doctrine of the Reagan administration, as enunciated from Washington and applied in El Salvador and Grenada and against Nicaragua, signifies that no country in this hemisphere can go its own way beyond the limits approved by Washington.

You can go to the right as much as you want: you can only be, at worst, a respected authoritarian.

You cannot go, even if democratically elected, too much to the left, for you then become a dangerous totalitarian.

Bi-polarism stalls the cultural, political and diplomatic contributions that the different nations and civilizations of our world, if left unhampered, would offer to everyone's benefit.

Three realities loom behind most immediate and identifiable conflicts: Latin America is a vital part of these three realities.

The first is the re-emergence of national cultures as expressions of dissatisfaction with the synthetic quality of ideologies and with the sacrifices imposed on cultural integrity by the indiscriminate rush — shared by the two world powers and their systems — towards the dogmatic values of future-oriented, modern progress.

The second is the internal tension, within the cultures themselves, between the technocratic, multinational demands of the so-called "global village" (in reality a very tiny if far-flung village containing the small minority of mankind that travels by Concorde, stays at a Western International Hotel and pays with a Diner's Club Card) and the assertions of local differences, regionalisms, decentralizations and sub-cultures — what we might call, in opposition to the global village, the "root metropolis," the familiar first city of mankind, the basic community of Emiliano Zapata and Huckleberry Finn.

The third is the affirmation of cultures — at the level of the region, national states or historical continents — as new centres of political and economic power.

This latter reality promises strife and tension in order to surpass the bi-polar hegemony in international relations in favour of a new multi-polar world. The dangers are great because never, since the end of World War Two, have the two strongest nations on our globe witnessed such an erosion of both their internal and external powers.

Their temptation to strike back at an ungrateful world in confusion, to prove their machismo, invoking in their efforts to reassert their power the danger of an endless void, can only be countered effectively by the political action of the emerging multi-polar powers: China and Japan, India and Islam, Latin America and black Africa, Western Europe now, and later, the two Europes in the process of becoming one in the twenty-first century. These are the multi-polar powers that must deflect East/West confrontation and offer flexible, regional or bilateral solutions instead of world-wide collision courses.

The second reality I referred to — the tension between multi-national and local demands — validates the importance of the national state as the historical filter, the centre of decisions, between multi-national power at the top and regional power at the bottom.

Countries such as mine, such as Mexico, clearly face this problem. The national state, long an established reality in France or England, now even, I suspect, a surpassed reality in the continental universe of the United States, is still a problematic goal for us in Mexico and in Latin America.

Many cultural initiatives originating from the lower strata have been postponed or even sacrificed in Mexico because the central state demands strength in order to apply its programmes nationally and defend itself from foreign pressures, particularly those from the United States. Conversely, Mexico — or Canada — cannot give in to demands for "enlightened interdependence" that actually would paralyse us in our present economic role, congeal us indefinitely as dependent suppliers.

The developing world, at this level, faces a vast dilemma:

How to achieve national unity without sacrificing local initiatives?

How to have both a strong national state and a free political system?

How, in effect, to have both material and political, cultural and, yes, spiritual development?

And finally, the first reality, the emergence of cultures as protagonists of history, proposes a re-elaboration of our civilizations in agreement with our deeper, not our more ephemeral, traditions. Dreams and nightmares, different songs, different laws, different rhythms, long-deferred hopes, different shapes of beauty, ethnicity and diversity, a different sense of time, multiple identities rising from the depths of the poly-cultural and multi-racial worlds of Africa, Asia and Latin America.

When the dust settles on the Central American conflict, we shall see that it was a chapter in the difficult and contradictory passage from a bi-polar to a multi-polar structure in world affairs.

Let me repeat this: China and Japan, India and Islam, Latin America and black Africa, Canada, Western Europe now and later the two Europes in the process of becoming one in the twenty-first century — these protagonists of a multi-polar world, no longer limited to domination by the United States and the Soviet Union, are inseparable from a process of re-emergence of cultures as protagonists of history.

This new reality, this new totality of humankind, presents enormous new problems, vast challenges to our imaginations. They open up the two-way avenue of all cultural reality: giving and receiving, selecting, refusing, recognizing, acting in the world: not being merely subjected to the world.

And responding to the dangers of the world, since all of us, everywhere, now face the same inescapable dilemma:

Since the time of Homer we have known that our personal future is a mask covering the face of death and that war and glory hasten the identification with death. Such is the message of *The Iliad*.

Now, for the first time in history, we know that we are capable not only of exterminating ourselves while at least leaving Nature to contemplate our folly, but that we are now capable of exterminating Nature herself, so that there shall be no further witnesses.

We thought that the future was ours. Now we wonder in terror if there shall be a future.

We live today. Tomorrow we shall have an image of today. We cannot ignore this, as we cannot ignore that the past was lived, that the origin of the past is the present: we remember here, today.

But we also imagine here, today. And we should not separate what we are able to imagine from what we are able to remember.

The knowledge of the past is the possibility of shaping an imperfect but reasonable future. If we understand that we made the past, we will not permit a future made without us or against us.

This is, I think, a valid statement for the work of the novelist as he evokes the past or imagines the future, but also remembers the future and imagines the past from this present in which all writing actually takes place.

For a writer does but conjugate the tenses and the tensions of time through verbal means, and his scope is dismally reduced if he, too, in order to synchronize with the ruling philosophy of modernity, must keep step with the indiscriminate rush towards the future, disregarding the only fulness in time: the present, where we remember and where we imagine.

Remember the future.

Imagine the past.

See the present and deal with it. It is a part of history.

Tomorrow it shall be the past, but so will tomorrow itself, today's future. Let us respect the times of mankind, not exacerbate and sacrifice them.

Only this interlocking activity permits me, for one, to understand my position and my work, as a Mexican national and as a Latin American writer, bound to a tradition and a hope inseparable from a history and a language, and as a writer convinced that there is no new creation without a living tradition, in the same way that there is no living present or possible future without a living past.

Let me again invoke, as I finish these Massey Lectures, the voices of culture.

Let me cling to the hope of the narrative voice: the hope that by telling the story of men and women, like Scheherezade, we are all deserving of one more night at the expense of one more tale.

If we are to have a future, it will depend on the growing presence of cultures long relegated to insignificance because they did not participate in the truths proper to the triumphalist West.

The plurality of the world's cultures organized as valid presences in a multi-polar world will dignify the contribution of untapped political, diplomatic, material and cultural resources to the solution of our vast international problems, for even if planetary destruction is avoided, a multitude of problems shall be waiting for the attention of political imagination in the internal spheres of all systems and most nations — waste, scarcity, the destruction of natural and human resources, poverty, education; and for the attention of diplomatic imagination in the international sphere — disarmament, economic co-operation, the conflicts of emerging nationhood in the Third World.

The security of each nation can only grow along with its self-respect and its self-assurance as its culture manifests itself freely, to the benefit of all.

A pluralistic internationalism cannot but reflect itself on the internal levels of democratic participation within each society.

A multi-polar, internationalist world would signify the affirmation of life by those who do not have the power of death.

Latin America, because of the wealth of its cultural continuity, can live with the future and with the past in its conflictive present.

The future and the past are but the actual value we all give to our present, where the times of mankind, being many, are one.

About the Author

Carlos Fuentes — novelist, diplomat, essayist, lecturer, art critic, and playwright — was born in Panama in 1928 and educated in Latin America, the United States, and Switzerland, where he worked with the International Law Commission and the International Labor Organization. In the 1970s, he served as Mexico's ambassador to France.

Carlos Fuentes' first novel, *Where the Air Is Clear*, was published in 1958 and he has since written more than twenty books. He has received many awards for his accomplishments, among them the Cervantes Prize in 1987. He divides his time between Mexico City and London, and lectures frequently in the United States.

The CBC Massey Lectures Series

Also available from House of Anansi Press in this prestigious series:

The Rights Revolution
Michael Ignatieff
0-88784-6564 (p) $16.95

The Triumph of Narrative
Robert Fulford
0-88784-6459 (p) $16.95

Becoming Human
Jean Vanier
0-88784-6319 (p) $16.95

The Elsewhere Community
Hugh Kenner
0-88784-6076 (p) $14.95

The Unconscious Civilization
John Ralston Saul
0-88784-586X (p) $14.95

On the Eve of the Millennium
Conor Cruise O'Brien
0-88784-5592 (p) $12.95

Democracy on Trial
Jean Bethke Elshtain
0-88784-5452 (p) $11.95

Twenty-First Century Capitalism
Robert Heilbroner
0-88784-5347 (p) $11.95

The Malaise of Modernity
Charles Taylor
0-88784-5207 (p) $14.95

Biology as Ideology
R. C. Lewontin
0-887845185 (p) $11.95

Prisons We Choose to Live Inside
Doris Lessing
0-88784-5215 (p) $9.95

The Politics of the Family
R. D. Laing
0-88784-5460 (p) $8.95

Nostalgia for the Absolute
George Steiner
0-88784-5940 (p) $17.95

Necessary Illusions
Noam Chomsky
0-88784-5746 (p) $24.95

Compassion and Solidarity
Gregory Baum
0-88784-5320 (p) $11.95

The Real World of Democracy
C. B. Macpherson
0-88784-5304 (p) $9.95

The Educated Imagination
Northrop Frye
0-88784-5983 (p) $12.95

The Real World of Technology Rev. Ed.
Ursula M. Franklin
0-88784-636X (p) $16.95

Designing Freedom
Stafford Beer
0-88784-5479 (p) $14.95